My First Book of KNOTS

Berndt Sundsten & Jan Jäger

A Beginner's Picture Guide

Sky Pony Press

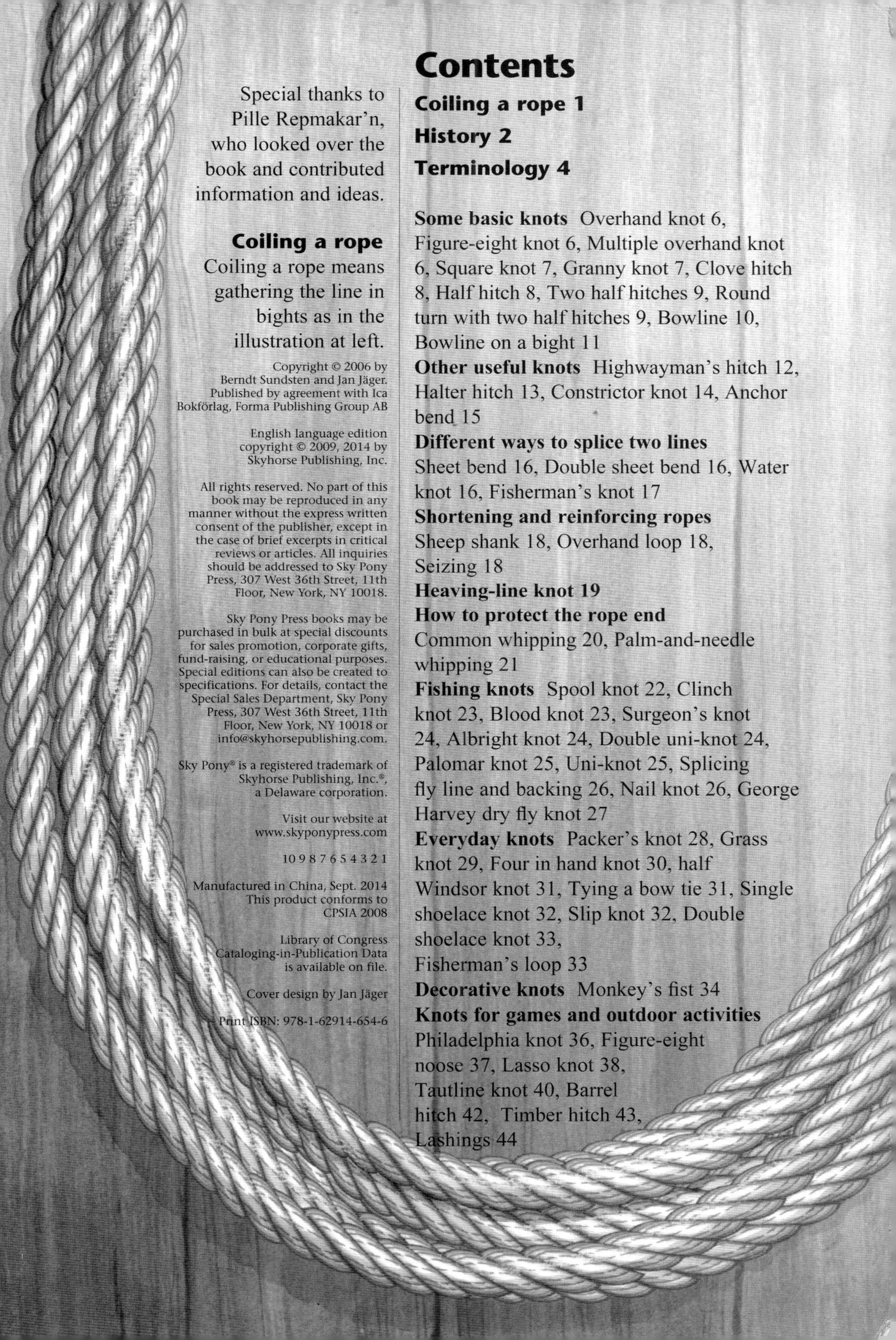

Special thanks to Pille Repmakar'n, who looked over the book and contributed information and ideas.

Coiling a rope

Coiling a rope means gathering the line in bights as in the illustration at left.

Copyright © 2006 by Berndt Sundsten and Jan Jäger. Published by agreement with Ica Bokförlag, Forma Publishing Group AB

English language edition copyright © 2009, 2014 by Skyhorse Publishing, Inc.

Sky Pony Press books may be purchased in bulk at special discounts for sales promotion, corporate gifts, fund-raising, or educational purposes. Special editions can also be created to specifications. For details, contact the Special Sales Department, Sky Pony Press, 307 West 36th Street, 11th Floor, New York, NY 10018 or info@skyhorsepublishing.com.

Sky Pony® is a registered trademark of Skyhorse Publishing, Inc.®, a Delaware corporation.

Visit our website at www.skyponypress.com

10 9 8 7 6 5 4 3 2 1

Manufactured in China, Sept. 2014 This product conforms to CPSIA 2008

Library of Congress Cataloging-in-Publication Data is available on file.

Cover design by Jan Jäger

Print ISBN: 978-1-62914-654-6

Contents

History

Knowing how to fasten something with a rope or how to make a knot is a useful skill to have. However, before you go on to learn different knots, here is a little background information.

The knot has been just as important for human evolution as the wheel. Technically, the knot is our oldest type of binding—that is, a tool for fastening and attaching different objects to one another. Over thousands of years, the technique of making knots has evolved, and in the past it was very important to be able to tie the right knots.

Knots have been used in many different areas. For example, they were used by the Inca in Peru to count people, weapons, and other objects. There are still people who tie string around their fingers in order to remember something important.

The word *knot* may be related to the word knob, possibly because *knots* tied at the end of a rope form a ball or *knob*. These knots were most likely made to prevent the rope from unraveling or so that it wouldn't glide through a hole.

The art of tying knots was at its peak when the great sailing ships sailed our waters. As a result, most knots have names related to the jobs they performed onboard ships. Many more knots were required at sea than on land. Today we don't have the same need to make knots. Still, when you do need to tie or fasten something, it's good to know some different kinds of knots.

With knots you can make loops, join ropes, or tie a line to or around something. You can also tie a decorative knot just because it looks nice.

All knots utilize friction, or the resistance created when two things glide against each other. The difference between a good knot and a bad one is that a good knot better utilizes friction so that it doesn't come undone. However, there are variations between different kinds of ropes. A good knot should also be possible to undo.

Even in everyday life it's worth knowing some effective and sturdy knots. Have you ever tried to make a pretty bow on a package, without success? There are knots for all occasions. They have a few different names that can be good to know.

Practice makes perfect

The old expression "practice makes perfect" is highly applicable to knots. Try making the knot by yourself until you can tie it without thinking about what you are doing. The best kind of memory is what's known as "muscle memory." An example: Once you've learned to ride a bike you will always remember how to do it. Remembering knots works the same way.

Now it's time to start practicing the knots you think will be useful for you. One suggestion: In the beginning it's easier if you use a rope the same width as your finger.

Terminology

The various parts of the rope and different knots have names or designations that are worth knowing.

The **working end** is the part of the rope you are using when tying a knot, while the **standing part** is either attached to something else or is not needed in order to make the knot.

The **rope end** is just as it sounds—the end of the rope.

Bight, round turn, and loop are three basic elements that are a part of all knot tying.

Bight. A bight is created when you bend the line to create a U shape.

Loop. If you continue to bend the line so that it crosses itself you get a loop. The "hole" in the middle is called the *eye*.

Round turn. If the loop is placed around an object, you get a round turn.

Set. A knot is called set when it is fully tightened.

Cordage

Cordage is all rope material (lines) used for boats, parachute cords, package wrapping, etc. It is made of fibers that may be natural or synthetic.

Laid cordage consists of smaller pieces called *strands* that are twisted around each other. Depending on which direction they are twisted around each other, they are called either Z-twist or S-twist. Z-twist, or right-laid, cordage is the most common.

Four-strand cordage has a middle section called the *core*.

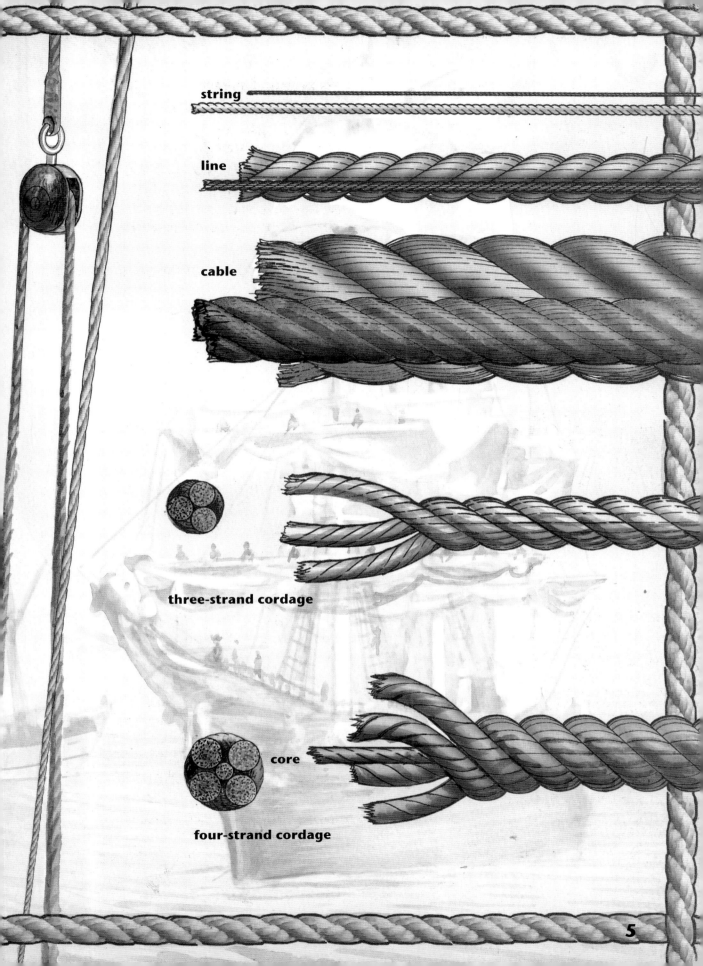

string

line

cable

three-strand cordage

core

four-strand cordage

Some basic knots

These basic knots are simple to tie and easy to undo.

Overhand knot

To prevent the end of a rope from unraveling, it's easiest to make an overhand knot. It is also used to make a stopper in a line.

Follow the illustration. Make a loop and poke the rope end through the eye. Now you've made the simplest and perhaps most common of all knots.

The figure-eight knot

This is an easy and effective knot that can be used, for example, to prevent a rope from gliding through the hole in a tarp.

How to tie it:

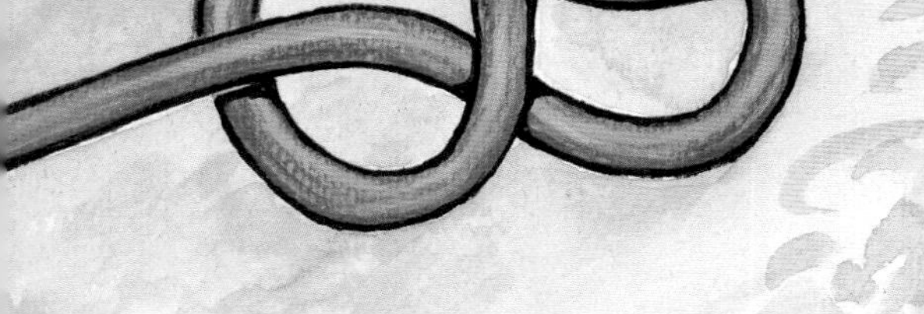

Multiple overhand knot

This knot makes a neat roll and can be used, for example, to create a better grip on a rope.

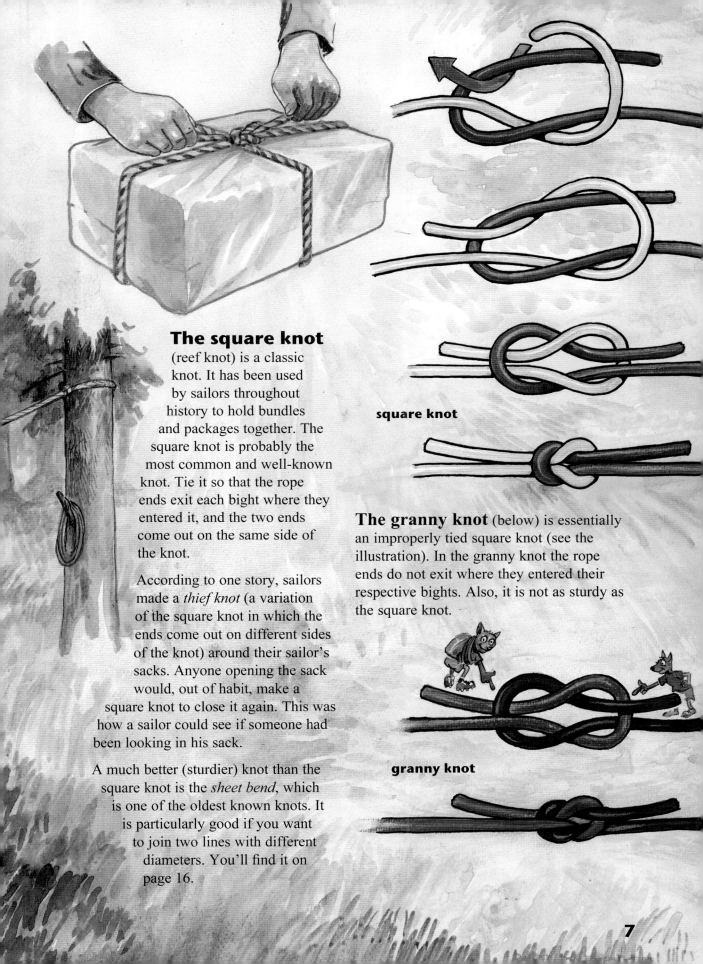

The square knot

(reef knot) is a classic knot. It has been used by sailors throughout history to hold bundles and packages together. The square knot is probably the most common and well-known knot. Tie it so that the rope ends exit each bight where they entered it, and the two ends come out on the same side of the knot.

According to one story, sailors made a *thief knot* (a variation of the square knot in which the ends come out on different sides of the knot) around their sailor's sacks. Anyone opening the sack would, out of habit, make a square knot to close it again. This was how a sailor could see if someone had been looking in his sack.

A much better (sturdier) knot than the square knot is the *sheet bend*, which is one of the oldest known knots. It is particularly good if you want to join two lines with different diameters. You'll find it on page 16.

square knot

The granny knot (below) is essentially

an improperly tied square knot (see the illustration). In the granny knot the rope ends do not exit where they entered their respective bights. Also, it is not as sturdy as the square knot.

granny knot

7

Hitches of different kinds are good for attaching a rope to an object, or tying things together. They also work well with other knots.

The clove hitch (above) is a great
knot when you need to fasten a line to a pole or other somewhat thicker object.

Half hitch
This is the simplest knot to use for fastening a line around an object. It works well as a temporary knot.

Two half hitches

This knot will hold even if the standing part varies between taut and loose.

1. Begin by laying a bight around the object.

2. Next, make a loop around the standing part with the rope end, which should come up through the bight.

3. Make another loop in the same direction around the standing part, and let the end come out between the two half loops.

4. Tighten the hitch by pulling on the standing part while holding your other hand around the two half hitches.

1 2 3 4

Round turn and two half hitches

This combination is very sturdy when, for example, you want to fasten a line around an object. This knot is quite easy to undo.

1 2 3 4 5

9

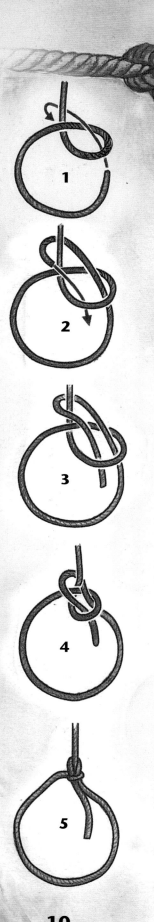

Bowline

With this basic knot you can make a strong, reliable noose of any size. The bowline is a knot that won't slip, and it can even be tied with one hand. This knot is also called the *rescue knot*.

Bowline

How to tie it:

1. Begin by making a loop in the line with the working end over the standing part, as shown in the illustration. Make the loop counterclockwise.

2. Next, poke the end through the loop from below.

3. Continue to wrap the end counterclockwise around the standing part and then poke it through the loop from above.

4. Now pull it tight . . .

5. . . . and the bowline is finished.

To remember how to make the bowline you can use this mnemonic: "A field mouse comes out of its hole, runs around the tree, and then goes back into its hole." You'll know just how to make a bowline.

The hole is the loop you make in the rope, the tree is the standing part of the rope, and the working end of the rope is the field mouse.

Bowline on a bight

The bowline on a bight is used, for example, to lift or lower someone during a rescue action. In such cases, the thickest line possible should be used. One of the loops should go under the person's rear end, and the other behind the back and under the armpits. The knot itself should be above the person's head. You can see how to make the knot at the bottom of the page.

If you want to make a swing you can do the following: Drill four holes in a piece of wood. Thread the rope through one of the holes from above, and through the other hole at the same end of the board from below. Fasten the rope end with a bowline. Do the same for the other end of the board.

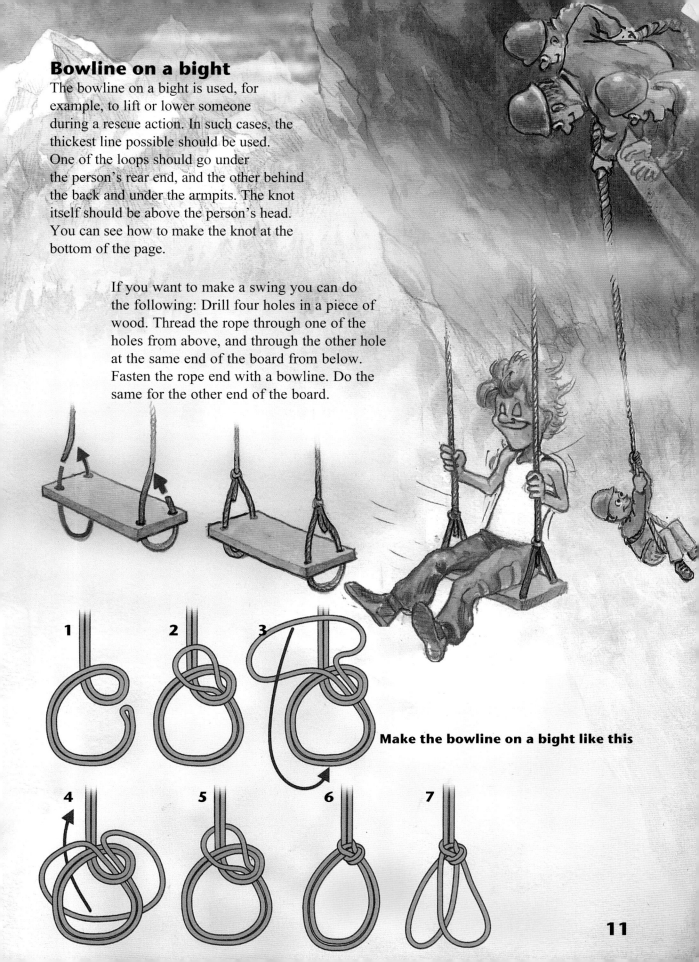

Make the bowline on a bight like this

1   2   3

4   5   6   7

Other useful knots

The highwayman's hitch is the perfect knot when you want to be able to undo the line quickly and smoothly. Tie the knot around a somewhat rounded object.

Here's how to tie a highwayman's hitch. Remember that the second bight (illustration 2) has to be made on the line that will hold the weight.

1

2

3

4

Pull in the direction of the arrow to quickly release the rope.

The halter hitch is another knot that is easy to quickly undo. Tie the knot in a loop or ring as shown in the illustrations below.

Pull here to quickly release the rope.

Constrictor knot

The constrictor is not only a knot, but also one of the names of the boa snake. It is a knot that, if pulled tight, really holds. The constrictor is often used when something needs to hold permanently.

It is useful if you want to fasten a rope around something. Don't pull it too tight; it can be difficult to undo.

Remember to never tie the knot around a body part.

Make the constrictor according to the illustrations to the left. The crosses mark where the object the knot is to be tied around should go in and out.

Undo the knot by pushing both rope ends into the knot at the same time.

You can even use it to tie a sack closed. Here's how to do it.

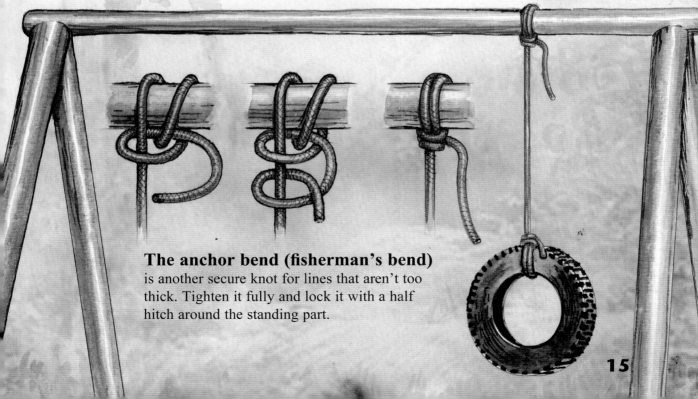

The anchor bend (fisherman's bend)
is another secure knot for lines that aren't too
thick. Tighten it fully and lock it with a half
hitch around the standing part.

Different ways to splice two lines

The sheet bend is a good and useful
knot when you want to join two lines.
It can be tied as a single or double knot.
You can use it if you want to join two
ropes when one has a fixed loop,
such as on a flag.

Sheet bend

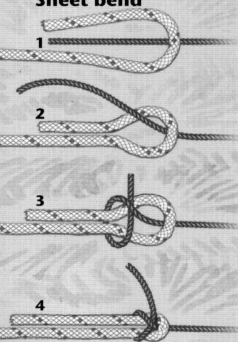

1

2

3

4

Double sheet bend

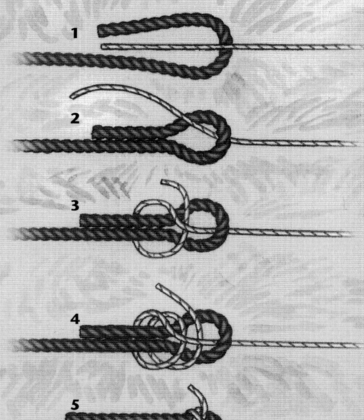

1

2

3

4

5

The sheet bend is one of our oldest
documented knots. It can be used
for ropes of different diameters. It
is also called the *weaver's knot* and
the *becket bend*.

The double sheet bend holds better than the
single version. It works well even if you tie
it using wet ropes.

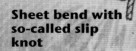

**Sheet bend with
so-called slip
knot**

The water knot (below) is suitable if
the rope you are using is relatively thin.

16

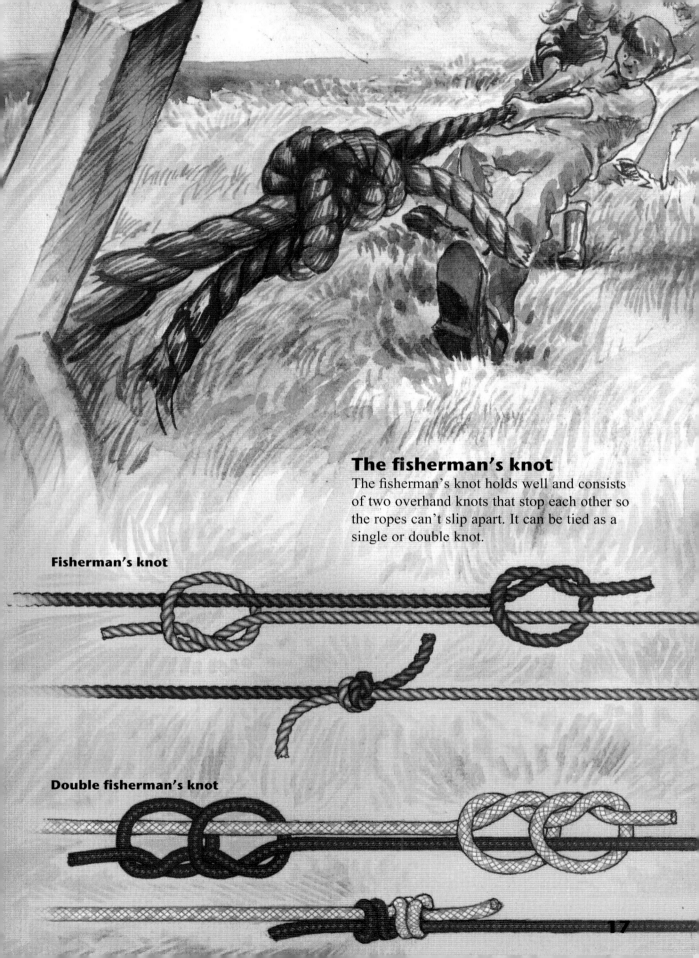

The fisherman's knot

The fisherman's knot holds well and consists of two overhand knots that stop each other so the ropes can't slip apart. It can be tied as a single or double knot.

Fisherman's knot

Double fisherman's knot

Shortening and reinforcing ropes

When you want to shorten a rope without cutting it, you can use the *sheep shank*. This knot can also be used to temporarily "isolate" damage to the rope. A version that can be used to quickly "repair" a damaged rope is the *overhand loop*. But remember that a knot always weakens a line.

Overhand loop

Sheep shank

Note that this knot works well when the rope is stretched at both ends. If you lash the parts together with a thinner line, as in illustration 5, the knot will hold better. Tie the sheep shank like this:

Seizing

To seize means to lash two parallel ropes to each other to hold them together.

round seizing

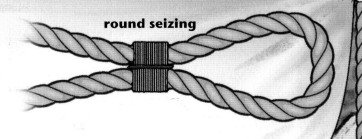

Heaving-line knot

The heaving-line knot is a good knot for when you want to put a stopper on a line or put weight on the line to be able to throw one of its ends. The knot is fairly easy to make and also easy to undo.

1. Begin by making a bight in the line.

2. Then wrap the working end once around the bight (one round turn).

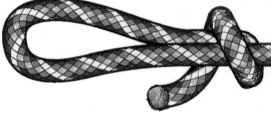

3. Continue by wrapping as many round turns (laps) as possible around the bight. Then stick the

working end through the bight and tighten it by holding onto the round turns while pulling on the standing part. The knot will come out better if you wrap the round turns at a bit of an angle.

The result is a slender and useful knot.

How to protect the rope end

There are a few different ways to prevent lines from unraveling. The easiest way is to make an overhand knot or a figure-eight knot; (see page 6). However, whipping the rope looks nicer.

Common whipping

1. Place a thin yarn or line alongside the rope so that the string makes a loop.

2. Wrap the yarn tightly around the rope and over the loop towards the end of the rope.

3. Continue so that the wrapping is at least as long as the rope is thick, but don't wrap over the whole loop. Tuck the end through the loop.

4. Pull on the end, marked **x**, so that the yarn is pulled under the wrapping and locks.

5. Finish by trimming the ends of the yarn with scissors.

Palm-and-needle whipping

This is considered the best type of whipping. If you have synthetic lines, this is the only way to prevent them from unraveling. To make the whipping you need a thin yarn or line to sew with.

1. Thread the yarn onto a needle, double it, and make a knot at the end.

2. Poke the needle between or through the strands as shown in the illustration and pull the knot into the rope.

3. Wrap tightly and evenly against the lay of the rope (opposite to the direction in which the rope strands are twisted). Wrap until the wrapping is approximately as wide as the rope is thick. Place the needle against the lay and stick it through or under a strand and out near the wrapping.

4. Let the yarn follow one of the notches between the rope strands toward the left. Poke the needle through the strand against the lay and close to the wrapping. Pull tight.

5. Let the yarn follow the next notch, but this time toward the right. Poke the needle through the strand and pull tight. Continue with the next notch, and so on.

6. Finish by poking the needle through the last strand, and then make a stopper knot in the yarn.

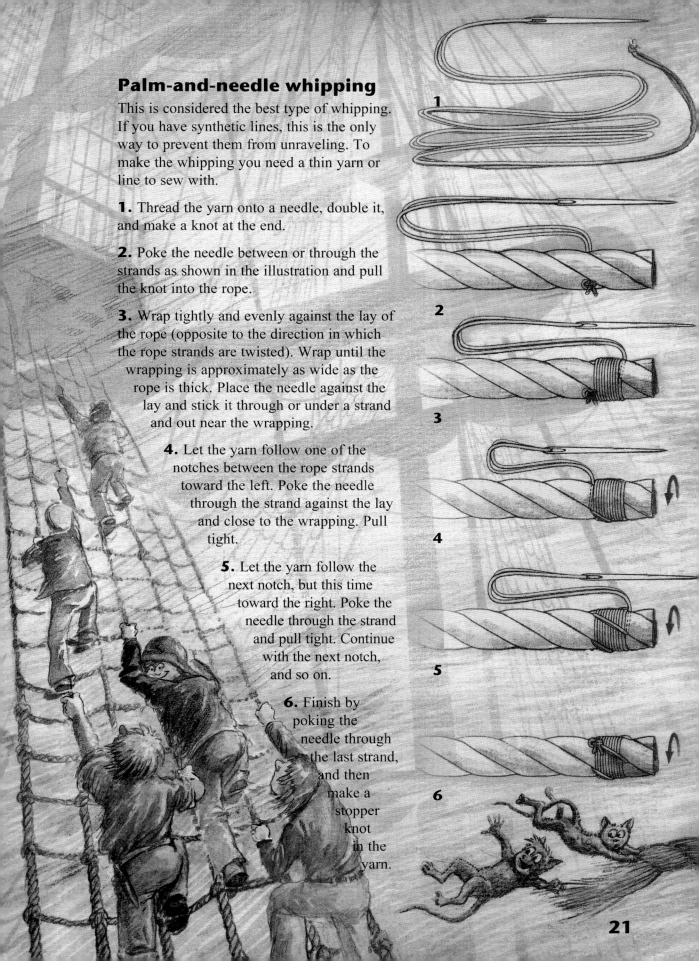

1

2

3

4

5

6

21

Fishing knots

It's important to know how to tie a few good knots if you're going on a fishing trip. They need to hold so that you can pull out the fish that bite. A poor knot greatly weakens the line. It's important to wrap the line the right number of times when you tie the knot.

Most knots are tied with nylon line. Always moisten the knot with saliva before pulling it tight. Knots made with nylon line should be pulled tight in one pull until they are fully tightened. Cut off the leftover line near the knot, and tug on the knot to test it. If a knot doesn't look good it's best to retie it.

Be careful! It's easy to cut yourself on the line or get a hook in your finger when you test the knot. To avoid this, you can put the fly/bait in a rod ring when you test the knot.

To start, here is a good and simple knot to fasten the fishing line with before spooling it onto the reel.

Spool knot

Here's how to tie a good spool knot. On casting and fly reels, you first place the end of the line around the spool of the reel and then tie the knot. On spinning reels you first make the loop, and then place it around the spool and pull it tight.

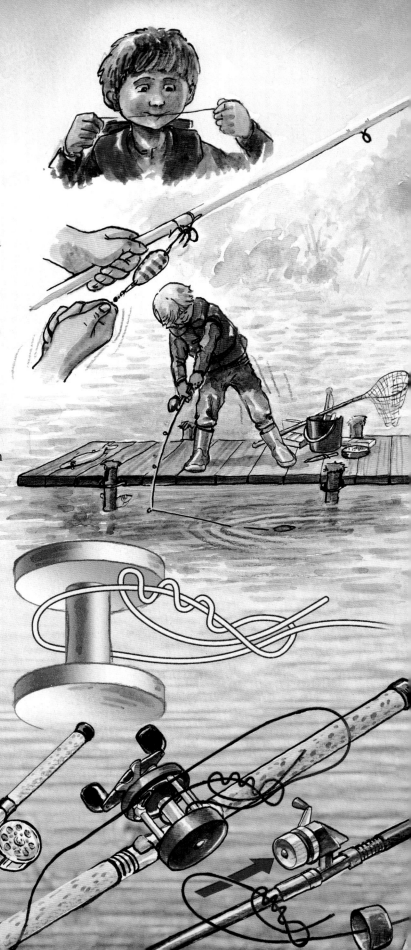

Clinch knot

To tie the line to the end of a rod for angling, for example, an *improved clinch* knot is great.

Wrap the line 4 times or more around it-self, and thread the end of the line through the outer loop and pull it tight. This will make the knot strong and will keep it from coming undone easily.

The improved clinch knot is also good for fastening a spoon bait or a spinner to the line. But, because the water makes the knot "slippery," you need to wrap the line at least 6 times around itself for the knot to hold. Make the knot on a bait hook with a swivel (see the illustration below). The swivel keeps the line from twining (twisting) when the bait and hook rotate.

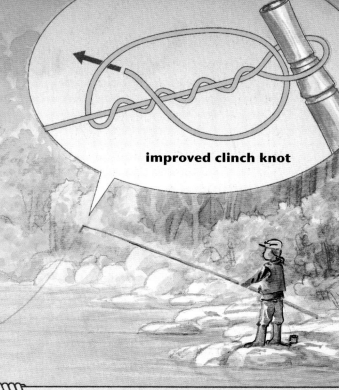

improved clinch knot

bait hook   **swivel**

Blood knot

The blood knot is the best and strongest knot for tying two lines together. If one of the lines is thin you should wrap it an extra time around.

Remember to moisten the knot with saliva before tightening firmly and evenly. Pull the knot tight from both directions in a single pull.

Here's how to tie the blood knot:

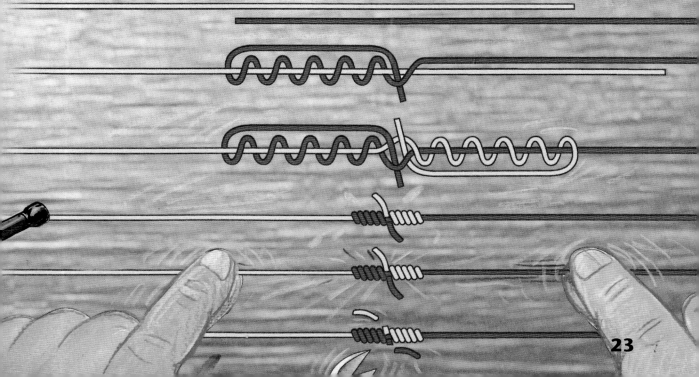

Spun lines are rigid and often require particular knots. You need these knots to tie nylon and spun lines together or to tie spun lines to each other.

The surgeon's knot can be used
to join two lines with the same or different diameters. It's especially good for fastening a tippet to a fly line.

The double uni-knot is particularly
good for braided lines or lines of different materials. It is tied like this:

Albright knot

The Albright special knot is used to join lines of different diameters and different materials, for example, a nylon line and spun line.

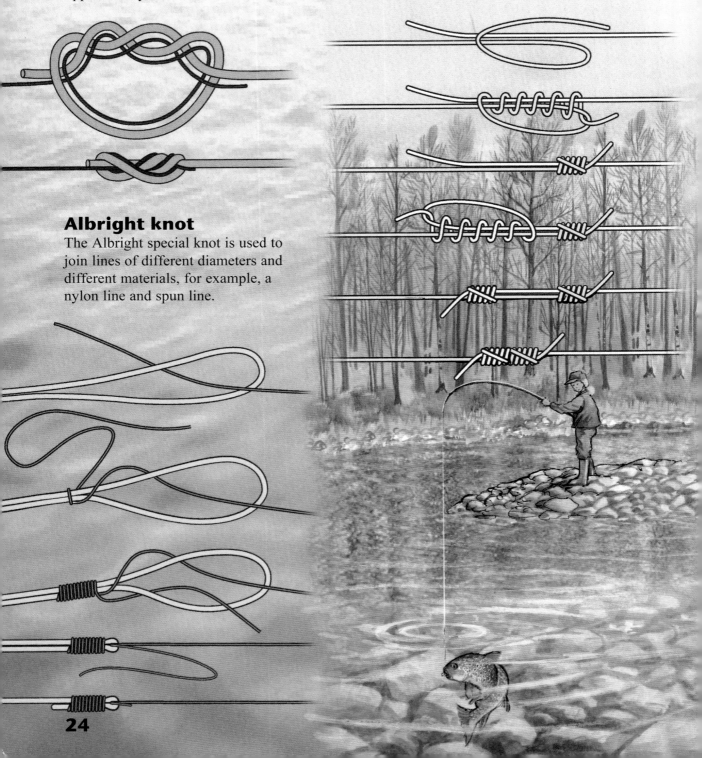

To fasten spoon bait, spinners, wobblers, or flies to the fishing line you need a few more knots.

The uni-knot (Duncan knot)

For the wobbler there is a special knot that gives it the right movement in the water. You tie it like this:

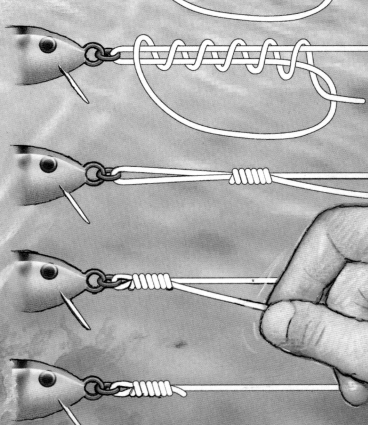

The palomar knot

This is a great bait knot for both spoon baits and flies. It is particularly good to use on Fireline lines.

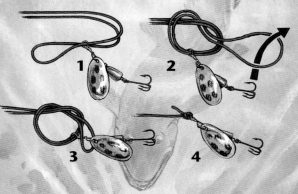

Tie it like this:

1. Fold the line in half and thread the loop through the eye of the bait/hook.
2. Follow the illustration by drawing the loop over the bait/hook.
3. Pull the knot tight.
4. Now you're ready to fish.

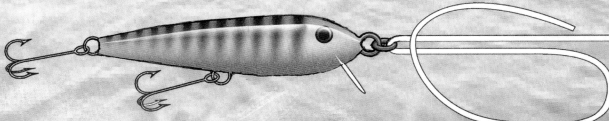

This page presents knots that are useful for fly-fishing.

Albright knot

Splicing fly line and backing

You need to join the backing to the fly line. There are two good ways. You can either make an *Albright knot* if the line is unbroken (see the illustration above) . . .

. . . or you can do as in the illustration to the right if the backing line is spun (made like a sock).

1. Cut the fly line at an angle.

2. Widen the backing and thread the fly line two–three centimeters (roughly 0.75– 1.25 inches) into the backing.

3. To strengthen the splice you can tie a nail knot (see below) around the backing and fly line. Or you can use a little special glue for knots and wind the knot with a thin line by using, for example, a spool holder (as used for fly binding) and spinning it around. The result will be a nice strong knot.

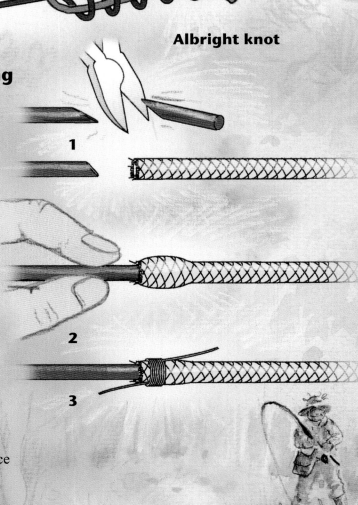

Nail knot

You can also use a nail knot to fasten the leader to the fly line. You need a tool such as a needle or a thin stick. Do as follows:

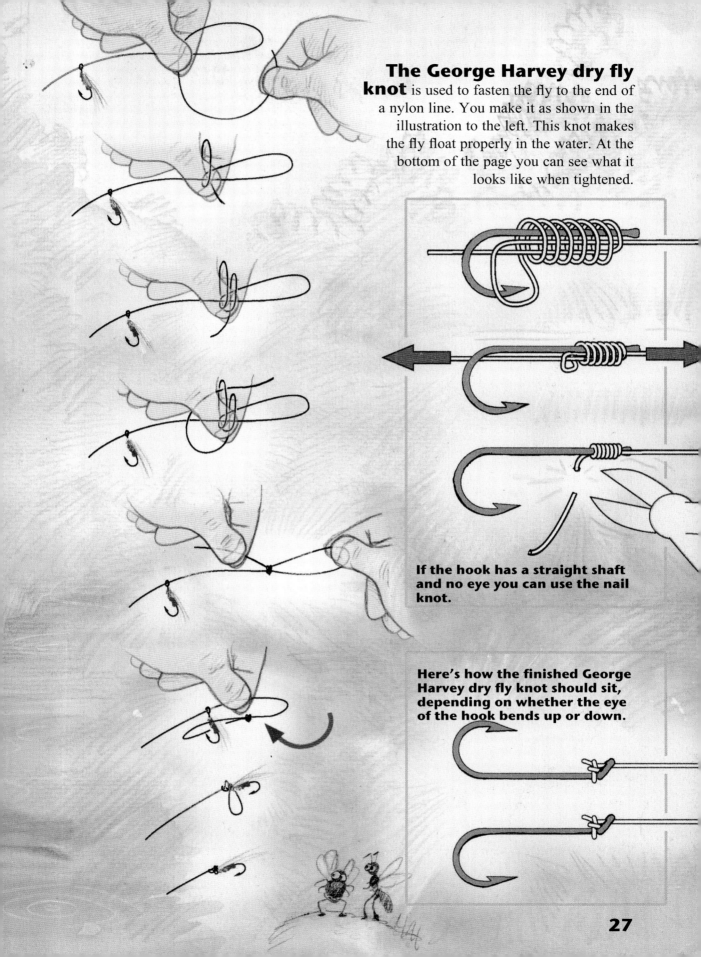

The George Harvey dry fly

knot is used to fasten the fly to the end of a nylon line. You make it as shown in the illustration to the left. This knot makes the fly float properly in the water. At the bottom of the page you can see what it looks like when tightened.

If the hook has a straight shaft and no eye you can use the nail knot.

Here's how the finished George Harvey dry fly knot should sit, depending on whether the eye of the hook bends up or down.

Everyday knots

The packer's knot is the perfect knot for tying around square packages, but it can also be used in other situations.

Begin by placing the string around the package. Follow the illustrations to lock the knot on the back side of the package.

Now you can stretch the string as much as you like, and the knot will lock itself when you stop stretching. Finish with a half hitch so that it stays nicely.

Grass knot

Choose this knot if you want to tie flat ribbons or straps around a package. The result looks great.

Sometimes it's necessary to wear a *tie or bowtie*. A neatly knotted tie makes a good impression. A properly made tie knot should not be pulled tight, and the tie should be long enough that its broad end is even with your belt. Here are two classic tie knots that can be used for most ties and are also good for bow ties. The first one, Four-in-hand, is suitable for all occasions.

Four in hand

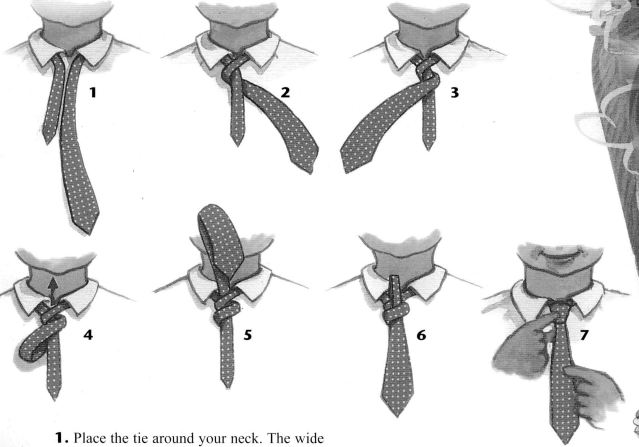

1. Place the tie around your neck. The wide end should hang much further down than the narrow end, so that you have something to make the tie knot with.

2. Take the wide end and follow the illustration.

3. Place the wide end over the narrow end.

4. Place the wide end under the beginnings of the knot.

5. Next, take the wide end from underneath and place it over the beginnings of your knot.

6. Stick the wide end of the tie under the topmost loop of the knot and pull it through.

7. Pull the knot together by pulling on the wide end of the tie with one hand, at the same time as you hold the knot and bring it together with the other hand.

Finally, thread the narrow end of the tie through the cloth label on the back of the wide end. This makes the narrow end of the tie less visible.

The half Windsor is a useful tie knot that is very good for silk ties. Make sure that the wide end hangs even lower than in the Four-in-hand knot. Tie it like this:

1. Loop the wide end of the tie over and under the narrow end.

2. Loop the wide end over the narrow one and then under the part of the tie that is around your neck.

3. Lift the wide end up and loop it under itself, as in the illustration.

4. Finally, pull the knot together as you did for the Four-in-hand knot.

Tie a bowtie like this:

1

2

3

4

5

6

7

8

9

Simple shoelace knot

A shoelace knot is a square knot with a double slip knot. A properly tied shoelace knot not only looks good but also holds well. If you pull the shoelace knot tight, you can use thicker shoelaces. Then they will hold without coming undone.

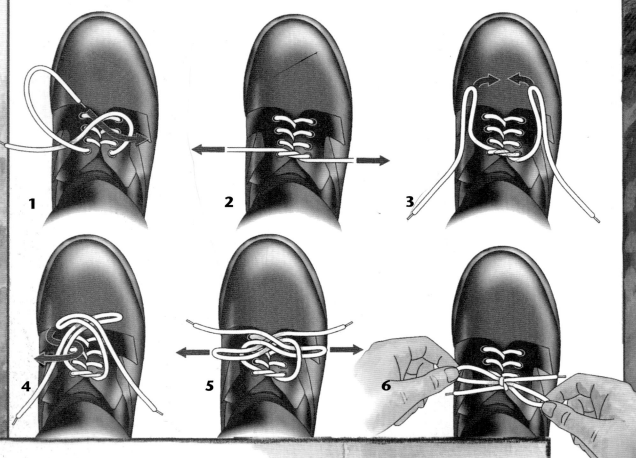

The slip knot is a knot that can be undone very quickly. The illustration shows a slip knot together with two round turns. The slip knot of slip knots is the *highwayman's hitch*, shown on page 12. The slip knot is a good knot if, for example, you want to tow a boat. The knot is easy to undo if a situation arises and you want to quickly release the boat being towed.

Pull here to undo the knot

Double shoelace knot

Synthetic shoelaces have a slipperier surface and can require an extra lock. In this case, you can make an identical knot on top of your first one, as shown in the illustrations. The double knot makes the shoelaces hold better.

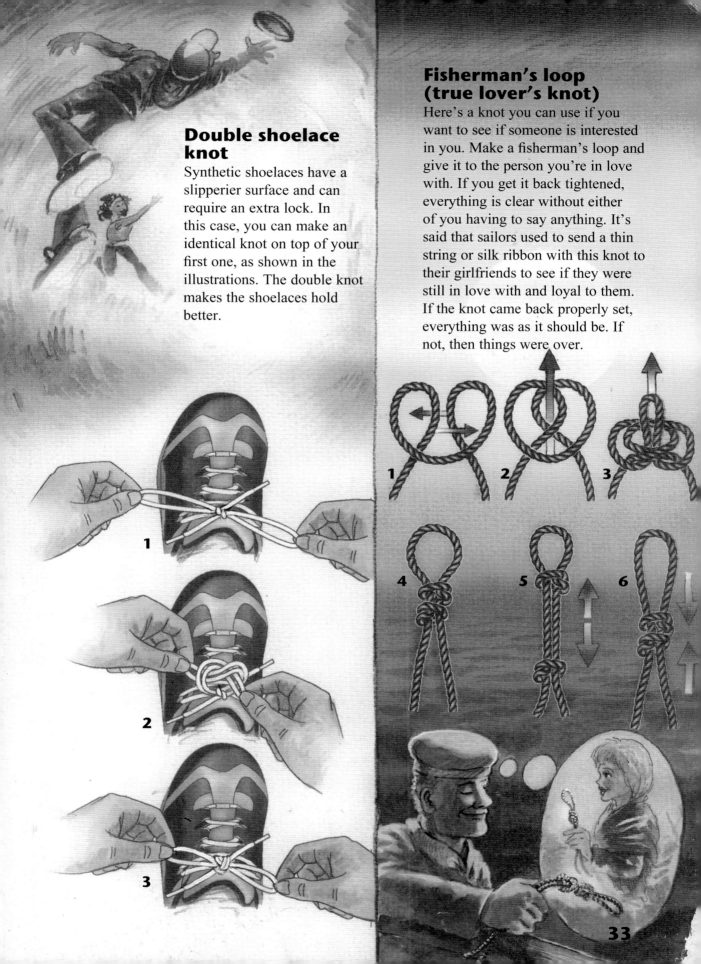

1

2

3

Fisherman's loop (true lover's knot)

Here's a knot you can use if you want to see if someone is interested in you. Make a fisherman's loop and give it to the person you're in love with. If you get it back tightened, everything is clear without either of you having to say anything. It's said that sailors used to send a thin string or silk ribbon with this knot to their girlfriends to see if they were still in love with and loyal to them. If the knot came back properly set, everything was as it should be. If not, then things were over.

1   2   3

4   5   6

Decorative knots

The monkey's fist is a decorative knot. You can put a wooden ball, for example, in the middle to get it to float. In order to make it even, you should tighten it a little bit at a time.

1. Make 3–4 round turns around your hand.

2. Next, make the same number of round turns around the first set of round turns.

3. Pull the working end that you are using through the first set of round turns.

4. Continue to draw the end down and around the second set of round turns and in through the first set.

5. Now it's time to place the object you've chosen inside the monkey's fist—a wooden ball, for example.

6. With the working end, continue around the second set of round turns (as shown in the illustration) until you have made the same number of round turns with the working end as in the previous sets.

7. Then, tuck in the trimmed end so that you get a nice-looking finish. It's easiest to tuck it in where the standing part of the rope sticks out of the knot.

8. Now you have to tighten each round of the knot so that it sets properly around the ball you placed in the middle.

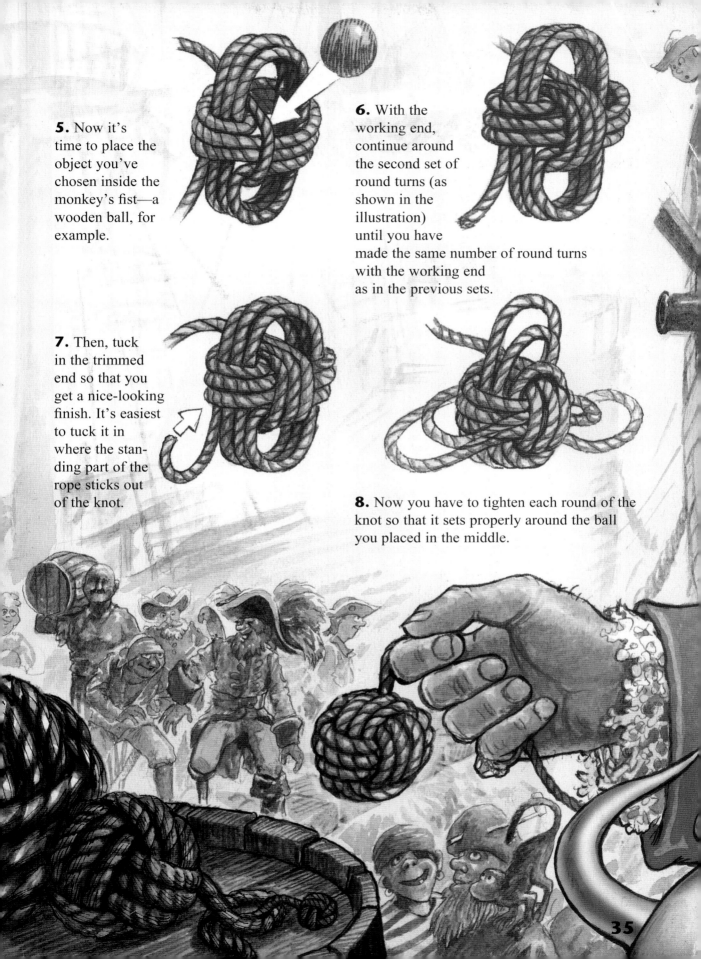

Knots for games and outdoor activities

The Philadelphia knot (fire-escape knot)

With the help of the Philadelphia knot, you can quickly and easily make a climbing rope. Learning to make a climbing rope used to be part of every firefighter's training. With this knot you will get a rope with a number of equally spaced overhand knots. Try making a climbing rope this way; it feels a bit like magic.

First, place the rope in "circles" on top of each other on the ground as shown in the illustration. This is called *coiling* the rope. Loop the rope in bights around your arm. Then, pull the working end in the back way and pull it tight so that you get overhand knots at even distances on the rope. It's easier to do with someone else.

Figure-eight noose
Make the knot according to the illustrations.

1

2

3

4

Lasso knot

A good lasso is 15–20 meters (50–65 feet) long and made of 5–10 mm (0.2.–0.4 inch) rigid plastic line or tarred hemp line.

To get a good and useable lasso, you should start by making the lasso knot. The knot is also called the *Honda knot*. You can make it as shown in the illustrations to the left.

5

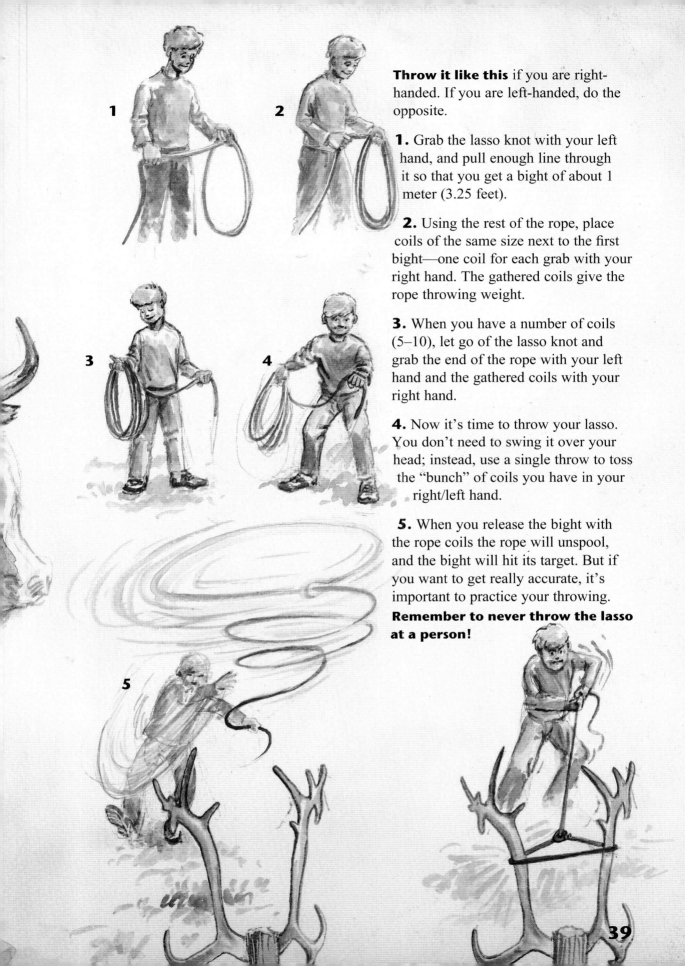

Throw it like this if you are right-handed. If you are left-handed, do the opposite.

1. Grab the lasso knot with your left hand, and pull enough line through it so that you get a bight of about 1 meter (3.25 feet).

2. Using the rest of the rope, place coils of the same size next to the first bight—one coil for each grab with your right hand. The gathered coils give the rope throwing weight.

3. When you have a number of coils (5–10), let go of the lasso knot and grab the end of the rope with your left hand and the gathered coils with your right hand.

4. Now it's time to throw your lasso. You don't need to swing it over your head; instead, use a single throw to toss the "bunch" of coils you have in your right/left hand.

5. When you release the bight with the rope coils the rope will unspool, and the bight will hit its target. But if you want to get really accurate, it's important to practice your throwing. **Remember to never throw the lasso at a person!**

Tautline knot

Here is a knot that you just have to know. What's so great about it is that it locks itself when it is weighted, but is easy to move when the weight is removed. It is also called the *midshipman's hitch* and the *rolling hitch*.

The tautline knot holds against sliding along the object on which it sits. For example, if the knot is tied around a mast or a pole, it can be weighted without slipping.

If you lay the line so that it goes around something or through a loop, and then tie the knot around its own line, you get a loop that is adjustable but will lock itself when weighted. The knot can be used, for example, in order to be able to adjust the lengths of tent ropes.

You can also use this knot to lift a long or large object to which you have several lines attached. Then, you can gradually lift a bit in every line and this way move the object to where you want it.

It's important to know in which direction the knot will be weighted so that you can tie it the right way.

Tie the knot like this:

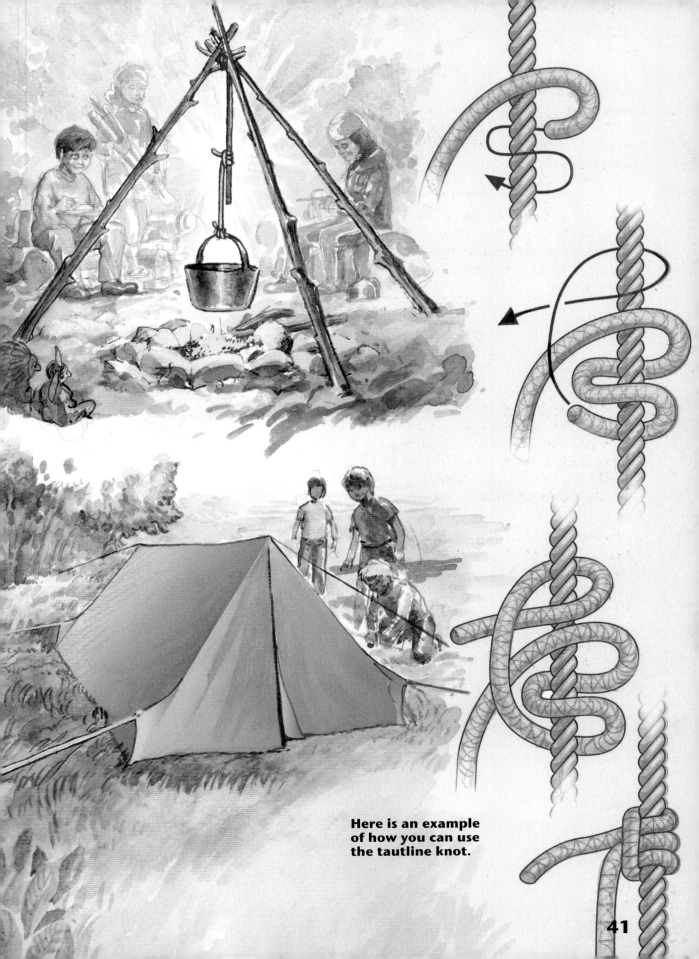

Here is an example of how you can use the tautline knot.

The barrel hitch

The barrel hitch is a knot that you can use to carry something that doesn't have handles. Imagine that you have a container or a can of paint that you need to carry.

1. Begin by drawing the rope under the container. Make sure there is a good length of rope on both sides.

2. Draw the rope up on both sides of the container. Wind the rope around itself over the container, in a so-called half knot, just as though you were tying your shoes.

3. Pull the half knot apart so that it forms two bights; fold these over the edges of the container.

4. Finally, tighten the rope and tie the loose ends at a suitable length with a square knot.

5. Now you have an ingenious and simple carrying device that works!

Timber hitch

Use this knot as a "starter knot" when you want to lash something. It can also be used if you want to drag something heavy.

If you don't have anything to carry your books with, you can do what people used to do: Tie a timber hitch around the books. Then you can easily carry them with you.

Make the timber hitch as shown in the illustrations to the right.

To drag a log, as shown in the picture below, you should use the timber hitch together with a half hitch (see the illustration). This makes it easier to drag the log.

Timber hitch, left, and **half hitch**, right.

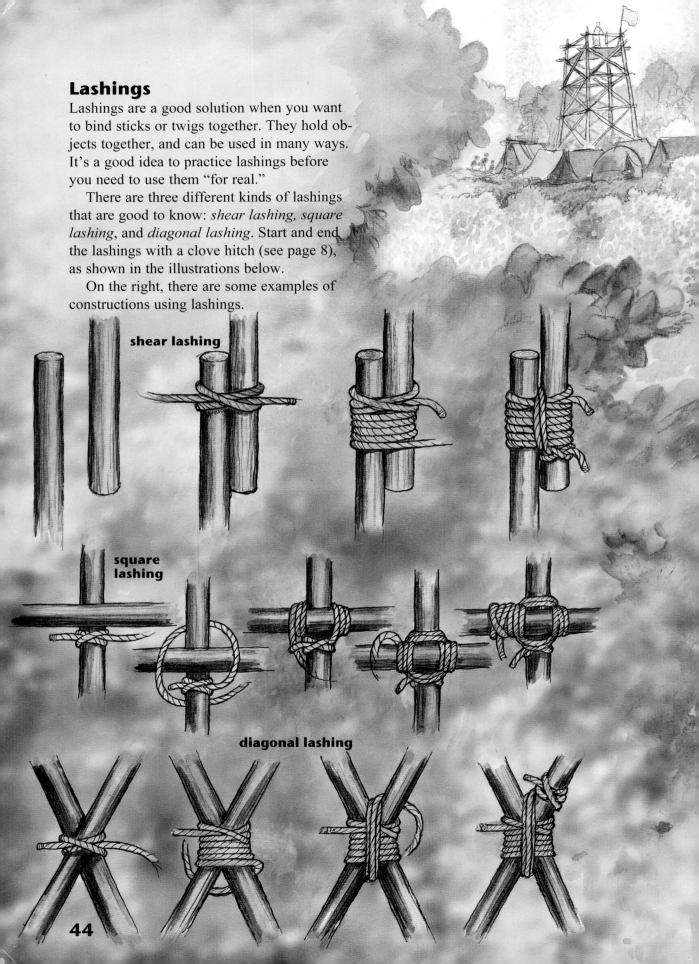

Lashings

Lashings are a good solution when you want to bind sticks or twigs together. They hold objects together, and can be used in many ways. It's a good idea to practice lashings before you need to use them "for real."

There are three different kinds of lashings that are good to know: *shear lashing, square lashing*, and *diagonal lashing*. Start and end the lashings with a clove hitch (see page 8), as shown in the illustrations below.

On the right, there are some examples of constructions using lashings.

shear lashing

square lashing

diagonal lashing